CW01426105

What Every Christian Should Know:

Essential Truths for Faith and Life

BRENDON NAICKER

Contents

Introduction

Christianity stands distinct among world religions with its unique understanding of salvation, which centres on God's sovereign grace rather than human merit or effort. Unlike many religious teachings that emphasise the necessity of adhering to specific principles or actions to attain a desired spiritual outcome, Christianity presents a profound message of grace and divine initiative.

The Foundation of Salvation

In Christian belief, salvation is entirely the result of God's sovereign choice and grace. It is not based on human achievements or righteousness but is a gift from God. This foundational truth is encapsulated in Ephesians 2:8-9: *"For by grace you have been saved through faith. And this is not your own doing; it is the gift of God, not a result of works, so that no one may boast."*

The Human Condition

Christianity teaches that all humans are inherently sinful and incapable of saving themselves. The Bible highlights this reality in Romans 3:10-12: *"None is righteous, no, not one; no one understands; no one seeks for God. All have turned aside; together they have become worthless; no one does good, not even one."* This recognition of human sinfulness underscores the need for divine intervention in the process of salvation.

The Role of Divine Grace

Salvation, according to Christianity, is initiated and accomplished by God. It involves recognising one's total dependence on God for salvation, trusting in His sovereign grace, and submitting to His lordship. This marks a profound transformation in a person's life. As 2 Corinthians 5:17 states, *"Therefore, if anyone is in Christ, he is a new creation. The old has passed away; behold, the new has come."* Through this transformation, individuals are regenerated by the Holy Spirit and enabled to live a life that honours and glorifies God.

Assurance and Purpose in Salvation

Embracing this understanding of salvation not only provides assurance of eternal life but also imbues believers with a sense of purpose and fulfilment. Christians believe they are called to love and serve God, seeking to glorify Him in all aspects of life. As 1 Corinthians 10:31 advises, *"So, whether you eat or drink, or whatever you do, do all to the glory of God."* This pursuit of living according to God's sovereign plan aligns believers with their ultimate purpose: to bring honour and praise to His name.

God's Sovereign Work

Ultimately, the decision to embrace the Christian faith and its understanding of salvation is seen as a result of God's sovereign work in the hearts of His people. It is not based on human choice or effort, but on God's graciousness. Romans 9:16 underscores this truth: *"So then it depends not on human will or exertion, but on God, who has mercy."*

Christianity offers a compelling and transformative perspective on salvation, emphasising God's sovereign grace and the believer's dependence on His mercy. This faith provides a profound sense of assurance, purpose, and fulfilment, guiding believers to live lives that glorify God. Through understanding and accepting this divine gift, individuals can experience the true essence of the Christian faith and its promise of eternal life with God.

Chapter 1: The Foundations of Christianity

Christianity, one of the world's major religions, traces its origins to the teachings and extraordinary acts of Jesus of Nazareth, who lived in the 1st century CE. Christians believe Jesus was born of a virgin, making him the incarnate Son of God, both fully divine and fully human. Jesus performed numerous miracles, including healing the sick, raising the dead, and calming storms, which demonstrated his divine authority and compassion.

Emerging from a milieu rich in Jewish religious tradition, Christianity quickly grew into a distinct faith with its own beliefs, practices, and texts, profoundly influencing Western civilisation and spreading globally. The Jewish historian Josephus Flavius, a non-Christian, wrote about Jesus, acknowledging him as a wise man who performed surprising feats and was called the Christ, providing external confirmation of Jesus' historical existence. The foundations of Christianity can be understood through its core beliefs, the life and teachings of Jesus, the role of the early church, and the development of its sacred texts.

Core Beliefs

At its heart, Christianity is centred on the belief in one God who exists as a Trinity: Father, Son (Jesus

Christ), and Holy Spirit. This doctrine of the Trinity is unique to Christianity and underscores the relationship and unity among the three persons of God. Christians believe that Jesus Christ is the incarnate Son of God, fully divine and fully human, who came to earth to offer salvation to humanity through his death and resurrection.

The concept of salvation is pivotal, emphasising that through Jesus' sacrificial death on the cross and subsequent resurrection, believers are offered forgiveness of sins and eternal life with God. This salvation is seen as a gift of grace, not earned by human efforts but received through faith in Jesus Christ. Central to this faith is the commandment to love God and neighbour, encapsulating the ethical teachings of Jesus.

Life and Teachings of Jesus

Jesus of Nazareth is the cornerstone of Christianity. Born around 4 BCE in Bethlehem and raised in Nazareth, Jesus began his public ministry around the age of 30. His teachings, parables, and miracles drew large crowds and sparked both admiration and controversy. Jesus preached about the Kingdom of God, emphasising repentance, forgiveness, and love. His radical teachings challenged the established religious authorities and norms of his day.

Jesus' crucifixion around 30 CE, ordered by the Roman governor Pontius Pilate, is seen by Christians as the fulfilment of divine prophecy and the means of human redemption. Christians believe that Jesus rose from the dead three days after his crucifixion, an event celebrated as Easter, which affirmed his divine nature and mission.

The Early Church

Following Jesus' resurrection and ascension, his disciples, notably the apostles Peter and Paul, began to spread his teachings. The early Christian community initially consisted of Jewish followers but soon expanded to include Gentiles (non-Jews). This expansion was significantly driven by Paul's missionary journeys and his letters (epistles) to various early Christian communities, which form a substantial part of the New Testament.

The early church faced persecution from both Jewish authorities and the Roman Empire. Despite this, Christianity grew rapidly, attracting converts from diverse backgrounds. The communal life of early Christians, characterised by shared resources, worship, and the breaking of bread (the Lord's supper), distinguished them from other religious groups.

Sacred Texts

The sacred texts of Christianity are the Bible, comprising the Old Testament and the New

Testament. The Old Testament, shared with Judaism, contains the Hebrew Scriptures, including the Torah, historical books, wisdom literature, and prophetic writings. These texts lay the groundwork for the Christian understanding of God's relationship with humanity and the anticipation of a Messiah.

The New Testament, written in the first century CE, includes the four Gospels (Matthew, Mark, Luke, and John), which recount the life, teachings, death, and resurrection of Jesus. Additionally, it contains the Acts of the Apostles, detailing the early church's history, the epistles, letters offering theological insights and practical guidance, and the Book of Revelation, an apocalyptic text.

Conclusion

Christianity's foundations are deeply rooted in the life and teachings of Jesus, the faith and practices of the early church, and the sacred texts that convey its doctrines and narratives. Over centuries, Christianity has developed various traditions, denominations, and theological interpretations, yet it remains unified in its core beliefs about Jesus Christ and his message of salvation. From its humble beginnings in a corner of the Roman Empire, Christianity has grown into a global faith, influencing countless lives and shaping human history in profound ways.

Chapter 2: What Makes Christianity Different

Christianity, while sharing some similarities with other major religions, has distinct beliefs and characteristics that set it apart. This exploration will highlight these differences, focusing on key theological, historical, and doctrinal aspects that uniquely define Christianity.

The Nature of God: The Trinity

One of the most distinguishing features of Christianity is the doctrine of the Trinity. Christians believe in one God who exists in three persons: Father, Son, and Holy Spirit. This concept profoundly shapes Christianity's understanding of God's nature and relationship with humanity. Unlike Christianity, Judaism and Islam emphasise the absolute oneness of God without a trinitarian distinction.

The Person of Jesus Christ

Central to Christianity is the belief in Jesus Christ as the incarnate Son of God. Christians hold that Jesus is both fully divine and fully human, a belief known as the hypostatic union. This contrasts sharply with other faiths:

Judaism views Jesus as a significant historical figure but not the Messiah or divine.

Islam recognises Jesus as a prophet but not as the Son of God and denies the crucifixion and resurrection.

Hinduism and Buddhism may respect Jesus as a wise teacher or enlightened being, but they do not accept him as the singular incarnation of the divine.

The Resurrection

The resurrection of Jesus is a foundational event in Christianity, seen as definitive proof of Jesus' divinity and the guarantee of eternal life for believers. This belief is unparalleled in other major religions. Islam denies the crucifixion and resurrection, asserting instead that Jesus was taken up to heaven by God. Other religions either do not emphasise resurrection in their teachings or have different interpretations of life after death.

Salvation by Grace Through Faith

Christianity teaches that salvation is a gift from God, received by grace through faith in Jesus Christ, not by human efforts or works: "*For by grace you have been saved through faith. And this is not your own doing; it is the gift of God, not a result of works, so that no one may boast*" (Ephesians 2:8-9). This concept is distinct from other religious systems:

Judaism emphasises a covenantal relationship with God, where adherence to the Law (Torah) is crucial.

Islam stresses submission to the will of Allah and adherence to the Five Pillars as essential for salvation.

Hinduism involves a cycle of karma and reincarnation, where actions in one life affect the next.

Buddhism focuses on achieving enlightenment through the Eightfold Path and escaping the cycle of rebirth.

The Concept of Grace

The Christian notion of grace—God's unmerited favour—is uniquely profound. Grace is the foundation of the Christian experience, emphasising that humans cannot earn salvation through their deeds but receive it freely through God's love: *"But God shows his love for us in that while we were still sinners, Christ died for us"* (Romans 5:8). This contrasts with merit-based systems in many other religions, where adherents seek to achieve favour or enlightenment through their actions and spiritual practices.

The Incarnation

Christianity uniquely claims that God became human in the person of Jesus Christ: *"And the Word became flesh and dwelt among us, and we have seen his glory, glory as of the only Son from the Father, full of grace and truth"* (John 1:14). This incarnation means that God entered human history, lived among us, experienced human suffering, and ultimately provided a way for humanity to be reconciled to Him. This personal and relational aspect of God distinguishes Christianity from other faiths, where gods are often seen as distant or only partially involved in the human experience.

The Role of the Bible

The Bible, comprising the Old and New Testaments, is considered the inspired and authoritative Word of God by Christians. It is unique in its cohesive narrative that spans creation, fall, redemption, and restoration. While other religions have sacred texts, the Bible's integrated story and its claims about Jesus as the fulfilment of Old Testament prophecies stand out: *"All Scripture is breathed out by God and profitable for teaching, for reproof, for correction, and for training in righteousness"* (2 Timothy 3:16).

The Ethical Teachings of Jesus

The ethical teachings of Jesus, particularly the Sermon on the Mount, emphasise love, forgiveness, and humility. These teachings challenge not only societal norms but also religious legalism. Jesus said, *"Love your enemies and pray for those who persecute you"* (Matthew 5:44), a radical and distinctive aspect of Christian ethics.

Conclusion

Christianity's unique beliefs about the nature of God, the person and work of Jesus Christ, the means of salvation, the concept of grace, and the ethical teachings of Jesus distinguish it from other faiths. These differences form the foundation of the Christian worldview, shaping its theology, practice, and the lives of its adherents. While respecting the value and insights of other religious traditions, Christianity offers a distinct and compelling narrative centred on a personal relationship with God through Jesus Christ.

Chapter 3: Evidence for the Existence of Jesus Christ

The existence of Jesus Christ is supported by a combination of historical, textual, and archaeological evidence. Scholars generally agree that Jesus of Nazareth was a historical figure, though interpretations of his life and significance vary. Here are the key pieces of evidence:

Biblical Accounts

The primary sources about Jesus' life and teachings come from the New Testament, particularly the Gospels of Matthew, Mark, Luke, and John. While these texts are religious documents, they also serve as historical sources written within a few decades of Jesus' lifetime.

Historical Context: The Gospels contain detailed descriptions of locations, cultural practices, and political situations consistent with the known history of 1st-century Judea.

Multiple Attestations: The Gospels were written by different authors at different times, providing independent attestations of Jesus' life.

Non-Christian Sources

Several non-Christian sources from antiquity mention Jesus, providing external validation of his existence.

Josephus (37-100 CE): In his work, *Antiquities of the Jews*, the Jewish historian Josephus refers to Jesus twice. One passage, known as the *Testimonium Flavianum,* describes Jesus as a wise man and a doer of wonderful works. Though some scholars debate the authenticity of parts of this passage, the consensus is that it contains a core authentic reference to Jesus.

- Source: Josephus, Antiquities of the Jews 18.63-64.

Tacitus (56-120 CE): The Roman historian Tacitus mentions Jesus in his *Annals*, written around 116 CE. He refers to Jesus' execution by Pontius Pilate during the reign of Tiberius, providing an important Roman perspective.

- Source: Tacitus, Annals 15.44.

Pliny the Younger (61-113 CE): In a letter to Emperor Trajan, Pliny the Younger, a Roman governor, describes early Christian worship practices and mentions Christ as the figure they worship.

- Source: Pliny the Younger, Letters 10.96-97.

Archaeological Evidence

While direct archaeological evidence for Jesus is scarce, discoveries have corroborated the historical context of the New Testament narratives.

The Pilate Stone: This inscription, found in Caesarea Maritima, confirms the existence of Pontius Pilate, the Roman prefect who ordered Jesus' crucifixion.

- Validation: The inscription reads, "Pontius Pilate, Prefect of Judea," directly tying a key figure in Jesus' story to the historical record.

The Caiaphas Ossuary: The ossuary (bone box) of Joseph Caiaphas, the high priest involved in Jesus' trial, has been discovered, affirming the New Testament account.

- Validation: The ossuary inscription identifies it as belonging to Caiaphas, providing archaeological evidence for his existence.

Scholarly Consensus

Most historians and scholars of antiquity agree on the historical existence of Jesus. For example, Bart D. Ehrman, a prominent New Testament scholar and agnostic, argues for Jesus' historicity based on the available evidence.

Books and Articles:

- *Bart D. Ehrman, *Did Jesus Exist? The Historical Argument for Jesus of Nazareth**
- *Ehrman provides a comprehensive overview of the evidence and scholarly arguments for the historical existence of Jesus.*
- *John P. Meier, *A Marginal Jew: Rethinking the Historical Jesus**
- *Meier's multi-volume work is a detailed scholarly investigation into the historical evidence for Jesus.*

Conclusion

The evidence for the existence of Jesus Christ includes biblical accounts, non-Christian historical sources, archaeological findings, and the consensus of modern scholarship. While the interpretations of Jesus' life and significance can vary, the convergence of multiple sources and types of evidence strongly supports the historical reality of Jesus of Nazareth. As the Gospels say, *"And the Word became flesh and dwelt among us, and we have seen his glory, glory as of the only Son from the Father, full of grace and truth"* (John 1:14), providing a powerful testament to the enduring influence of Jesus' life and teachings.

Chapter 4: Claims Made by Jesus and Proofs of His Validity

Jesus of Nazareth made several significant claims during his ministry that are foundational to Christian belief. These claims encompass his identity, authority, and purpose. Below, we explore these claims and provide evidence supporting their validity.

Claim to Divinity:

Jesus claimed to be divine, the Son of God.

Biblical Evidence:

- John 10:30: *"I and the Father are one."*
- John 14:9: *"Anyone who has seen me has seen the Father."*
- Mark 14:61-62: *During his trial, when asked if he is the Messiah, the Son of the Blessed One, Jesus responds, "I am."*

Validation:

- Fulfilment of Prophecies: Jesus fulfilled numerous Old Testament prophecies regarding the Messiah, such as Isaiah 7:14 (virgin birth), Micah 5:2 (birth in Bethlehem), and Isaiah 53 (suffering servant).

- Early Christian Writings: Early Christian texts and creeds affirm Jesus' divinity (e.g., Philippians 2:6-11).

Claim to Forgive Sins:

Jesus claimed the authority to forgive sins, which is a divine prerogative.

Biblical Evidence:

- Mark 2:5-7: *Jesus forgives the sins of a paralytic, leading onlookers to question, "Who can forgive sins but God alone?"*
- Luke 7:48-49: *Jesus tells a sinful woman, "Your sins are forgiven."*

Validation:

- Miracles as Signs: Jesus often performed miracles in conjunction with forgiving sins, providing a tangible sign of his authority. For example, in Mark 2, after forgiving the paralytic's sins, Jesus heals him to demonstrate his authority (Mark 2:10-12).

Claim to Be the Messiah:

Jesus claimed to be the promised Messiah, the anointed one prophesied in the Hebrew Scriptures.

Biblical Evidence:

- John 4:25-26: Jesus explicitly identifies himself as the Messiah to the Samaritan woman at the well.
- Matthew 16:16-17: Peter declares Jesus to be the Messiah, and Jesus affirms this revelation.

Validation:

- Triumphal Entry: Jesus' entry into Jerusalem on a donkey (Matthew 21:1-11) fulfils Zechariah 9:9, a messianic prophecy.
- Resurrection: The resurrection is seen as the ultimate validation of Jesus' messianic claims. It confirmed his power over death and his divine mission.

Claim to Be the Way, the Truth, and the Life

Jesus claimed to be the exclusive path to God.

Biblical Evidence:

- John 14:6: *"I am the way and the truth and the life. No one comes to the Father except through me."*

Validation:

- Transformation of Lives: The profound transformation of Jesus' followers, many of whom faced persecution and martyrdom, supports the authenticity and power of his teachings.

- Consistency of Teachings: Jesus' teachings consistently pointed to his unique role in salvation, supported by his actions and the continuity of the New Testament narrative.

Claim to Perform Miracles

Jesus claimed to perform miracles as signs of his divine authority and compassion.

Biblical Evidence:

- Various passages: Healings (Mark 5:21-43), control over nature (Matthew 14:22-33), exorcisms Luke 8:26-39), and raising the dead (John 11:1-44).

Validation:

- Eyewitness Testimony: The Gospels contain numerous accounts of miracles witnessed by many people, including sceptics and opponents.
- External Sources: Non-Christian sources like Josephus also mention Jesus as a doer of "wonderful works" (Antiquities 18.63-64).

Proofs of Jesus' Validity

Historical Reliability of the Gospels

The Gospels are considered reliable historical documents by many scholars due to their early composition, internal consistency, and corroboration by external sources.

- Dating of Texts: The Gospels were written within a few decades of Jesus' life, allowing for the preservation of accurate oral traditions.
- Archaeological Corroboration: Archaeological findings, such as the Pilate Stone and the Caiaphas Ossuary, support the historical context of the Gospel narratives.

Eyewitness Testimonies

The New Testament authors, particularly the apostles, claimed to be eyewitnesses of Jesus' life, death, and resurrection (e.g., 1 John 1:1-3, 2 Peter 1:16-18). Their willingness to suffer and die for their testimony adds credibility to their claims.

Impact on History

The rapid growth of the early Christian church, despite intense persecution, and the lasting impact of Jesus' teachings on ethics, law, and society provide indirect evidence of the profound truth and transformative power of his message.

Conclusion

The claims made by Jesus about his divinity, authority to forgive sins, messianic role, and unique path to God are supported by a combination of biblical evidence, fulfilment of prophecies, corroboration by non-Christian sources, and the profound impact on his followers and history. These elements collectively validate the authenticity of Jesus' claims and underscore his significance in human history.

Chapter 5: Validity of the Resurrection of Jesus Christ

The resurrection of Jesus Christ is a foundational claim of Christianity, and its validity is supported by several lines of evidence. Here are the key arguments and sources that provide a convincing case for the resurrection:

Historical Reliability of the Gospels

The Gospels of Matthew, Mark, Luke, and John provide detailed accounts of the resurrection. These texts are considered reliable historical documents by many scholars for several reasons:

- Early Composition: Most scholars agree that the Gospels were written within a few decades of Jesus' death, close enough to the events to ensure reliable transmission of eyewitness testimony.
- Consistency: The core details of the resurrection narrative are consistent across all four Gospels, despite differences in secondary details, which suggests independent accounts of the same event.

Eyewitness Testimonies

The New Testament contains numerous claims of eyewitnesses who encountered the risen Jesus:

- 1 Corinthians 15:3-8: Paul lists several individuals and groups who saw the risen Jesus, including Peter, the apostles, over 500 brethren at once, James, and Paul himself. This letter is one of the earliest Christian writings, dated around AD 55, within 25 years of the resurrection.
- Gospel Accounts: Mary Magdalene, the other women at the tomb, the apostles, and other disciples reported seeing and interacting with the risen Jesus (e.g., Matthew 28, Mark 16, Luke 24, John 20-21).

Empty Tomb

The empty tomb is a crucial piece of evidence:

- Multiple Attestations: The empty tomb is mentioned in all four Gospels, indicating a strong tradition that the tomb was indeed found empty.
- Women as Witnesses: The Gospels report that women were the first to discover the empty tomb. In the cultural context of the time, women's testimony was not highly regarded, making it unlikely that the Gospel writers would invent such a story unless it were true.
- Counter-Arguments: Early Jewish polemics acknowledged the empty tomb by claiming that the disciples stole Jesus' body (Matthew

28:11-15), indirectly affirming the tomb was empty.

Transformation of the Disciples

The dramatic transformation of the disciples from fearful deserters to bold proclaimers of the resurrection supports the truth of their testimony:

- Behaviour Change: After Jesus' crucifixion, the disciples were disheartened and in hiding (John 20:19). Following the resurrection appearances, they became bold witnesses, willing to face persecution and martyrdom.
- Spread of Christianity: The rapid growth of the early Christian church, despite severe persecution, is difficult to explain without the disciples' genuine belief in the resurrection.

Paul's Conversion

Paul (formerly Saul of Tarsus) was a zealous persecutor of Christians who became a devoted apostle after encountering the risen Jesus:

- Radical Transformation: Paul's conversion is well-documented in his letters and in the Acts of the Apostles. His immediate change from persecutor to leading missionary suggests a profound experience.
- Eyewitness Claim: Paul claims to have seen the risen Jesus, an experience he describes in 1 Corinthians 15:8 and Galatians 1:11-17.

Empty Tomb and Resurrection in Early Preaching

The resurrection was a central theme in the early Christian preaching as recorded in the Acts of the Apostles:

- Acts 2:22-32: Peter's Pentecost sermon focuses on Jesus' resurrection, witnessed by the apostles.
- Acts 4:10: The apostles consistently preached the resurrection as the basis of their faith and message.

Conclusion

The validity of the resurrection of Jesus Christ is supported by multiple lines of evidence: the historical reliability of the Gospel accounts, numerous eyewitness testimonies, the empty tomb, the transformation of the disciples, Paul's dramatic conversion, and the centrality of the resurrection in early Christian preaching. These elements collectively provide a strong and convincing case for the resurrection as a historical event.

Chapter 6: What is the Church?

The concept of the church is central to Christianity, representing both a physical gathering of believers and a spiritual body united by faith in Jesus Christ. People meet, preach, and sing in church for various reasons, reflecting the multifaceted nature of Christian worship and community-building. Here's an exploration of the concept of the church and the biblical basis for gathering, preaching, and singing:

The Church: A Spiritual Community

Definition: The term "church" comes from the Greek word "*ekklesia*," which means "assembly" or "gathering." In Christian theology, the church refers to the global body of believers in Jesus Christ, as well as local congregations or assemblies.

Purpose

- Worship: The church gathers to worship God, expressing reverence, adoration, and gratitude through prayer, song, and sacraments.
- Fellowship: Believers come together to build relationships, offer support, and encourage one another in their faith journey.
- Teaching: Preaching and teaching in the church provide spiritual guidance, instruction in biblical truths, and application to daily life.

- Mission: The church is called to share the message of salvation, engage in acts of service, and fulfil the Great Commission to make disciples of all nations.

Biblical Support for Gathering, Preaching, and Singing

Gathering

"And let us consider how we may spur one another on toward love and good deeds, not giving up meeting together, as some are in the habit of doing, but encouraging one another—and all the more as you see the Day approaching." (Hebrews 10:24-25).

"For where two or three gather in my name, there am I with them." (Matthew 18:20).

Preaching and Teaching

"Preach the word; be prepared in season and out of season; correct, rebuke and encourage—with great patience and careful instruction." (2 Timothy 4:2)

"On the first day of the week we came together to break bread. Paul spoke to the people and, because he intended to leave the next day, kept on talking until midnight." (Acts 20:7)

Singing and Worship

> *"Speaking to one another with psalms, hymns, and songs from the Spirit. Sing and make music from your heart to the Lord." (Ephesians 5:19).*

> *"Let the message of Christ dwell among you richly as you teach and admonish one another with all wisdom through psalms, hymns, and songs from the Spirit, singing to God with gratitude in your hearts." (Colossians 3:16).*

Conclusion

The church serves as a spiritual home for believers, providing a place for worship, fellowship, teaching, and mission. Gathering together allows Christians to support and encourage one another, preach and teach biblical truths, and express their devotion to God through singing and worship. These practices are rooted in biblical principles and reflect the essential elements of Christian community and faith.

Chapter 7: The Understanding of Humanity from a Biblical Perspective?

The understanding of humanity is deeply rooted in the teachings of the Bible, emphasising both the dignity and the depravity of human beings. This perspective is shaped by the doctrines of creation, fall, redemption, and restoration, reflecting key theological principles from the Protestant Reformation.

Creation: Imago Dei (Image of God)

Dignity and Purpose*:* Humans are created in the image of God (imago Dei), which gives them inherent dignity, value, and purpose.

> *"Then God said, 'Let us make man in our image, after our likeness. And let them have dominion over the fish of the sea and over the birds of the heavens and over the livestock and over all the earth and over every creeping thing that creeps on the earth.' So God created man in his own image, in the image of God he created him; male and female he created them" (Genesis 1:26-27).*

This means humans possess attributes that reflect God's character, such as rationality, morality, creativity, and relationality. They are also given the responsibility to steward and care for creation.

The Fall: Sin and Depravity

The fall of Adam and Eve brought sin and corruption into the human condition. The doctrine of total depravity means that every aspect of human nature is tainted by sin, and humans are incapable of saving themselves.

> *"As it is written: 'None is righteous, no, not one; no one understands; no one seeks for God. All have turned aside; together they have become worthless; no one does good, not even one'"* *(Romans 3:10-12).*

> *"Therefore, just as sin came into the world through one man, and death through sin, and so death spread to all men because all sinned"* *(Romans 5:12).*

Total depravity does not mean that humans are as bad as they could be, but rather that sin affects every part of a person: their mind, will, emotions, and body.

Redemption: Grace and Salvation

The Bible emphasises God's sovereignty in the process of salvation. Humans are utterly dependent on God's grace for their redemption, which is accomplished through the atoning work of Jesus Christ.

> *"For by grace you have been saved through faith. And this is not your own doing; it is the gift of God, not a result of works, so that no one may boast" (Ephesians 2:8-9).*

> *"For those whom he foreknew he also predestined to be conformed to the image of his Son, in order that he might be the firstborn among many brothers. And those whom he predestined he also called, and those whom he called he also justified, and those whom he justified he also glorified" (Romans 8:29-30).*

This salvation is not based on human effort but is a result of God's initiative and mercy.

Restoration: New Creation in Christ

Sanctification and Glorification: Believers are progressively sanctified (made holy) through the work of the Holy Spirit and will ultimately be glorified in the new creation.

> *"Therefore, if anyone is in Christ, he is a new creation. The old has passed away; behold, the new has come" (2 Corinthians 5:17).*

> *"And I am sure of this, that he who began a good work in you will bring it to completion at the day of Jesus Christ" (Philippians 1:6).*

In this restored state, humans will fully reflect the image of God, free from sin and its effects, living in perfect communion with God.

Conclusion

The biblical perspective on humanity reveals a complex being created in the image of God, fallen into sin, redeemed by grace through Christ, and ultimately restored to a state of glory. This understanding emphasises the profound dignity and value of humans, their complete dependence on God for salvation, and the transformative power of God's grace in their lives. These doctrines underscore the commitment to the sovereignty of God and the centrality of Christ in the story of humanity.

Chapter 8: What is Salvation and Why Does Humanity Need Saving?

Salvation is a central theme in Christian theology, referring to the deliverance from sin and its consequences through faith in Jesus Christ. Salvation is understood as a work of God's grace from beginning to end. Here's an exploration of what salvation is, why humanity needs it, and what we are saved from, supported by scripture and other theological verifications.

What is Salvation?

Salvation in Christian theology encompasses several aspects:

- **Justification:** Being declared righteous before God.
- **Sanctification:** The process of becoming holy.
- **Glorification:** The final state of believers in eternal life.

"If you confess with your mouth that Jesus is Lord and believe in your heart that God raised him from the dead, you will be saved. For with the heart one believes and is justified, and with the mouth one confesses and is saved" *(Romans 10:9-10).*

> *"For by grace you have been saved through faith. And this is not your own doing; it is the gift of God, not a result of works, so that no one may boast" (Ephesians 2:8-9).*

Salvation is a gift from God, received through faith in Jesus Christ, not by human effort.

Why Does Humanity Need Saving?

Depravity and Sin:

All humans are born in a state of sin due to the Fall (Genesis 3). This concept is known as total depravity, meaning that sin affects every part of a person, rendering them incapable of saving themselves.

> *"For all have sinned and fall short of the glory of God" (Romans 3:23).*

> *"Therefore, just as sin came into the world through one man, and death through sin, and so death spread to all men because all sinned" (Romans 5:12).*

Separation from God:

Sin causes separation from God, leading to spiritual death and eternal separation from His presence.

> *"But your iniquities have made a separation between you and your God, and your sins have*

hidden his face from you so that he does not hear" (Isaiah 59:2).

"For the wages of sin is death, but the free gift of God is eternal life in Christ Jesus our Lord" (Romans 6:23).

Chapter 9: From What Does Salvation Save Us?

Wrath of God

Salvation saves us from the righteous wrath of God against sin. God's holiness and justice require that sin be punished.

> *"Since, therefore, we have now been justified by his blood, much more shall we be saved by him from the wrath of God" (Romans 5:9).*

> *"Whoever believes in the Son has eternal life; whoever does not obey the Son shall not see life, but the wrath of God remains on him" (John 3:36).*

Sin and Its Power

Salvation delivers us from the power of sin, enabling us to live righteous lives through the Holy Spirit.

> *"We know that our old self was crucified with him in order that the body of sin might be brought to nothing, so that we would no longer be enslaved to sin. For one who has died has been set free from sin" (Romans 6:6-7).*

> *"For freedom Christ has set us free; stand firm therefore, and do not submit again to a yoke of slavery" (Galatians 5:1).*

Eternal Death

Salvation rescues us from eternal death and grants us eternal life with God.

> *"For God so loved the world, that he gave his only Son, that whoever believes in him should not perish but have eternal life" (John 3:16).*

> *"He will wipe away every tear from their eyes, and death shall be no more, neither shall there be mourning, nor crying, nor pain anymore, for the former things have passed away" (Revelation 21:4).*

Conclusion

Salvation is the process by which God delivers believers from sin, its consequences, and eternal separation from Him. Humanity needs saving because of the pervasive nature of sin, which incurs God's wrath, enslaves individuals, and leads to spiritual and eternal death. Salvation, as revealed in scripture, is a gift of grace through faith in Jesus Christ, who bore the penalty for sin and grants eternal life to those who trust in Him. This comprehensive deliverance encompasses justification, sanctification, and ultimate glorification, reflecting the fullness of God's redemptive plan.

Chapter 10: Heaven and Hell - Their Reality and Criteria for Eternal Destinies

In Christian theology, heaven and hell are considered real, eternal destinations for human souls after death. The belief in heaven and hell is rooted in the teachings of Jesus and the Apostles, as recorded in the Bible. Here's an explanation of these concepts, the criteria for ending up in either place, and a clarification that Christian theology does not support a dualistic worldview.

Heaven

Nature of Heaven:

Heaven is depicted as the dwelling place of God, a place of eternal joy, peace, and fellowship with God. It is described as a place where there is no more suffering, sin, or death, and where believers experience the fullness of God's presence.

> *"My Father's house has many rooms; if that were not so, would I have told you that I am going there to prepare a place for you? And if I go and prepare a place for you, I will come back and take you to be with me that you also may be where I am." (John 14:2-3).*

> *"And I heard a loud voice from the throne saying, 'Look! God's dwelling place is now among the people, and he will dwell with them. They will be his people, and God himself will be with them and be their God. He will wipe every tear from their eyes. There will be no more death' or mourning or crying or pain, for the old order of things has passed away.'"* (Revelation 21:3-4).

Hell

Nature of Hell:

Hell is depicted as a place of eternal separation from God, characterised by suffering and regret. It is described as a place of judgment and punishment for sin.

> *"Then he will say to those on his left, 'Depart from me, you who are cursed, into the eternal fire prepared for the devil and his angels.'"* (Matthew 25:41).

> *"They will be punished with everlasting destruction and shut out from the presence of the Lord and from the glory of his might."* (2 Thessalonians 1:9).

Criteria for Eternal Destinies

Faith in Jesus Christ:

The primary criterion for entering heaven, according to Christian belief, is faith in Jesus Christ as Lord and Savior. This faith involves repentance of sin and trust in Jesus' atoning sacrifice on the cross.

"For God so loved the world that he gave his one and only Son, that whoever believes in him shall not perish but have eternal life." (John 3:16).

"If you declare with your mouth, 'Jesus is Lord,' and believe in your heart that God raised him from the dead, you will be saved. For it is with your heart that you believe and are justified, and it is with your mouth that you profess your faith and are saved." (Romans 10:9-10).

Rejection of Christ:

Conversely, rejection of Christ and His offer of salvation results in eternal separation from God, which the Bible describes as hell.

"Whoever believes in him is not condemned, but whoever does not believe stands condemned already because they have not believed in the name of God's one and only Son." (John 3:18).

"Then they will go away to eternal punishment, but the righteous to eternal life." (Matthew 25:46).

No Dualism in Christian Theology

Definition of Dualism:

Dualism is the belief that two fundamentals, opposing forces (such as good and evil) are equally powerful and eternal.

Christian Rejection of Dualism:

Christianity rejects dualism, affirming that God is the sovereign Creator and Sustainer of all things. Evil, including Satan and hell, is a created reality and not an eternal or equal counterpart to God. God's sovereignty ensures that evil is ultimately subordinate to God's will and will be defeated.

> *"I am the Lord, and there is no other; apart from me there is no God. I will strengthen you, though you have not acknowledged me, so that from the rising of the sun to the place of its setting people may know there is none besides me. I am the Lord, and there is no other. I form the light and create darkness, I bring prosperity and create disaster; I, the Lord, do all these things." (Isaiah 45:5-7).*

> *"And the devil, who deceived them, was thrown into the lake of burning sulphur, where the beast and the false prophet had been thrown. They will be tormented day and night for ever and ever." (Revelation 20:10).*

Conclusion

Heaven and hell are real, eternal destinations in Christian theology, with the criteria for entering heaven being faith in Jesus Christ and repentance of sins. Conversely, rejection of Christ results in eternal separation from God in hell. Christianity rejects dualism, affirming God's ultimate sovereignty over all creation, including the eventual defeat of evil. This theological framework emphasises the necessity of a relationship with Jesus Christ for eternal life with God.

Chapter 11: What Must I Do to Be Saved According to Biblical Teachings?

Salvation is at the heart of Christian theology, representing the deliverance from sin and its consequences through faith in Jesus Christ. This chapter explores the biblical understanding of salvation and the steps towards assurance.

Repent and Believe in Jesus Christ

Repentance:

Repentance involves a deep sorrow for sin, a turning away from it, and a commitment to live in obedience to Christ. It is not merely feeling sorry for wrongdoing but a genuine change of heart and mind that leads to a transformation of life.

- Acts 2:38: After Peter's sermon on the day of Pentecost, he exhorted the people to repent and be baptised in the name of Jesus Christ for the forgiveness of sins. Repentance here signifies a radical turning away from a life of rebellion against God to a life of submission and obedience to Him.
- 2 Corinthians 7:10: Paul distinguishes between godly sorrow and worldly sorrow. Godly sorrow leads to repentance that results

in salvation and leaves no regret, whereas worldly sorrow leads to death. True repentance is marked by a sincere change in attitude and behaviour towards God and others.

Faith in Jesus Christ:

Faith is central to salvation—it is trusting in Jesus Christ alone for the forgiveness of sins and eternal life. This faith involves both belief in who Jesus is (the Son of God) and what He has done (died and rose again for our salvation).

- John 3:16: This famous verse encapsulates the essence of saving faith. Believing in Jesus Christ means trusting that God sent His Son into the world out of love, so that whoever believes in Him will not perish but have eternal life.
- Romans 10:9-10: Paul outlines the confession of faith required for salvation. It involves believing in Jesus with the heart (trusting in His atoning sacrifice) and confessing with the mouth that Jesus is Lord (acknowledging His authority and lordship over one's life).

Understand That Salvation is By Grace Through Faith

Grace Alone:

Salvation is not something we can earn or deserve through our own efforts or good works. It is entirely a gift from God, given out of His love and mercy towards sinful humanity.

- Ephesians 2:8-9: These verses emphasise that salvation is by grace through faith, and not by works. This is crucial because it highlights that our salvation is initiated and completed by God's unmerited favour, not by anything we can achieve on our own.

Faith Alone:

Faith is the instrument through which we receive God's grace. It is not faith plus works, but faith alone in the finished work of Jesus Christ on the cross. This faith involves trust in Christ's redemptive work for the forgiveness of sins and reconciliation with God.

- Romans 3:28: Paul's assertion here is clear: we are justified (declared righteous before God) by faith apart from the works of the law. This underscores that our standing before God is based entirely on our faith in Jesus Christ, not on our own moral or religious efforts.

Receive the Assurance of Salvation

Inner Witness of the Holy Spirit:

The Holy Spirit plays a vital role in assuring believers of their salvation. He testifies with our spirit that we are children of God, providing a deep-seated conviction and confidence in our relationship with God.

- Romans 8:16: This verse highlights the personal and intimate aspect of assurance. The Holy Spirit affirms within us our adoption as God's children, reinforcing our identity and security in Christ.

Changed Life:

Genuine faith results in a transformed life characterised by the fruit of the Spirit and growing holiness. This transformation is evidence of the Holy Spirit's work in the believer's heart and life.

- Galatians 5:22-23: The fruit of the Spirit— love, joy, peace, patience, kindness, goodness, faithfulness, gentleness, and self-control—are indicators of genuine faith and life in Christ. These qualities progressively manifest as the believer grows in their relationship with God.
- 2 Corinthians 5:17: Paul describes the profound change that occurs in a person who becomes a follower of Christ. They become a

new creation, with old sinful patterns of life passing away and new godly desires and attitudes taking their place.

Perseverance of the Saints:

True believers are kept secure in their salvation by God's preserving grace. They continue to trust in Christ and live in obedience to Him, sustained by the Holy Spirit.

- Philippians 1:6: Paul expresses confidence in God's faithfulness to complete the work He has begun in believers. This assurance of perseverance is grounded in God's sovereignty and His commitment to those who belong to Him.
- John 10:28-29: Jesus promises eternal security to His followers. No one can snatch them out of His hand or the Father's hand, underscoring the certainty of their salvation and the protection provided by God.

How Do I Know I Am Saved?

Trust in Christ Alone*:* The journey towards assurance begins with genuine trust in Jesus Christ as Lord and Saviour. It involves wholeheartedly relying on His sacrifice for forgiveness and acceptance by God.

Evidence of the Holy Spirit's Work*:* Look for the inner testimony of the Holy Spirit in your heart, confirming your status as a child of God and sealing your relationship with Him.

Fruit of the Spirit: Examine your life for the presence and growth of spiritual fruit. These qualities—love, joy, peace, patience, kindness, goodness, faithfulness, gentleness, and self-control—are evidence of the Holy Spirit's transformative work in your life.

Love for God and Others: A genuine love for God and a growing love for others are natural outcomes of a heart transformed by God's grace and a sign of authentic faith.

- 1 John 4:7-8: John emphasises the connection between knowing God and loving others. Genuine love is evidence of our new life in Christ and our relationship with Him.

Perseverance in Faith: Endurance in faith through trials and challenges is a mark of true discipleship. It demonstrates reliance on God's strength and commitment to following Jesus despite difficulties.

Alignment with Scripture: Regularly examine your beliefs and experiences in light of biblical teachings on salvation and Christian living. Scripture serves as the ultimate authority and guide for understanding and confirming our faith.

Conclusion

Biblical teachings affirm that salvation is a gift from God, received through repentance and faith in Jesus Christ alone. Assurance of salvation comes through the inner witness of the Holy Spirit, a transformed life marked by the fruit of the Spirit, and the believer's perseverance in faith. This perspective underscores God's grace as the foundation of salvation and emphasises the role of faith and the Holy Spirit in the believer's journey of assurance and sanctification.

Chapter 12: What It Is to Pray, How to Pray, and Why It Matters?

What is Prayer?

Prayer, in the Christian faith, is a profound means of communicating with God. It encompasses various forms, including adoration, confession, thanksgiving, and supplication. Through prayer, believers express their thoughts, emotions, and desires to God, seeking His guidance, help, and presence in their lives.

> *"Do not be anxious about anything, but in everything by prayer and supplication with thanksgiving let your requests be made known to God. And the peace of God, which surpasses all understanding, will guard your hearts and your minds in Christ Jesus." (Philippians 4:6-7).*

> *"Rejoice always, pray without ceasing, give thanks in all circumstances; for this is the will of God in Christ Jesus for you." (1 Thessalonians 5:16-18).*

Prayer is a holistic practice that involves acknowledging God's sovereignty, seeking His forgiveness, expressing gratitude, and presenting our needs and the needs of others to Him.

How to Pray

Adoration:

Adoration is the act of praising God for who He is—His holiness, love, power, and wisdom. It is recognising and declaring God's supreme worth and majesty.

> *"Great is the LORD, and greatly to be praised, and his greatness is unsearchable." (Psalm 145:3).*

Adoration shifts our focus from ourselves to God, reminding us of His greatness and our dependence on Him.

Confession:

Confession involves admitting our sins and shortcomings to God, seeking His forgiveness and cleansing. It is an essential aspect of maintaining a right relationship with God.

> *"If we confess our sins, he is faithful and just to forgive us our sins and to cleanse us from all unrighteousness." (1 John 1:9).*

Through confession, we acknowledge our failures and receive God's grace, which restores our fellowship with Him.

Thanksgiving:

Thanksgiving is expressing gratitude for God's blessings, provision, and answered prayers. It acknowledges God's goodness and faithfulness in our lives.

"Continue steadfastly in prayer, being watchful in it with thanksgiving." (Colossians 4:2).

A thankful heart recognises God's past faithfulness and fosters trust in His future provision.

Supplication:

Supplication involves presenting our requests to God, asking for His help, guidance, and intervention in specific areas of our lives and the lives of others.

"First of all, then, I urge that supplications, prayers, intercessions, and thanksgivings be made for all people." (1 Timothy 2:1).

Supplication is an act of humility, recognising our needs and God's ability to meet them.

Model of Prayer - The Lord's Prayer:

Jesus provided a model for prayer known as the Lord's Prayer, which encompasses these elements.

"Pray then like this: 'Our Father in heaven, hallowed be your name. Your kingdom come,

your will be done, on earth as it is in heaven. Give us this day our daily bread, and forgive us our debts, as we also have forgiven our debtors. And lead us not into temptation, but deliver us from evil.'" (Matthew 6:9-13).

The Lord's Prayer serves as a comprehensive guide, incorporating adoration, submission to God's will, requests for provision, forgiveness, and protection.

Why Pray?

Communion with God:

Prayer encourages a personal relationship with God, allowing believers to draw near to Him and experience His presence. It is a means of developing intimacy with God.

> *"Draw near to God, and he will draw near to you." (James 4:8).*

Through prayer, we cultivate a deeper connection with God, sensing His presence and guidance in our lives.

Dependence on God:

Prayer acknowledges our dependence on God for all things, reminding us that He is the source of our provision, strength, and guidance.

"Trust in the LORD with all your heart, and do not lean on your own understanding. In all your ways acknowledge him, and he will make straight your paths." (Proverbs 3:5-6).

By turning to God in prayer, we affirm our reliance on His wisdom and provision rather than our own.

Alignment with God's Will:

Through prayer, believers seek to understand and align their lives with God's will, surrendering their own desires and accepting His plans.

"And this is the confidence that we have toward him, that if we ask anything according to his will he hears us." (1 John 5:14).

Prayer helps us discern God's will and aligns our hearts with His purposes, ensuring our desires and actions reflect His will.

Peace and Comfort:

Prayer provides peace and comfort, especially in times of anxiety, uncertainty, and distress. It is a means of experiencing God's peace, which surpasses all understanding.

"Do not be anxious about anything, but in everything by prayer and supplication with thanksgiving let your requests be made known to God. And the peace of God, which surpasses

all understanding, will guard your hearts and your minds in Christ Jesus." (Philippians 4:6-7).

In prayer, we find solace and reassurance in God's presence, knowing He is in control.

Intercession for Others:

Prayer allows believers to intercede for others, lifting their needs and seeking God's intervention in their lives.

> "Praying at all times in the Spirit, with all prayer and supplication. To that end, keep alert with all perseverance, making supplication for all the saints." (Ephesians 6:18).

Intercessory prayer reflects our love and concern for others, entrusting their needs to God's care.

Spiritual Growth and Maturity:

Prayer contributes to spiritual growth, helping believers to mature in their faith, develop a deeper understanding of God, and become more Christ-like.

> "And so, from the day we heard, we have not ceased to pray for you, asking that you may be filled with the knowledge of his will in all spiritual wisdom and understanding, so as to walk in a manner worthy of the Lord, fully pleasing to him: bearing fruit in every good work and increasing in the knowledge of God." (Colossians 1:9-10).

Regular prayer nurtures spiritual growth, encouraging a deeper relationship with God and a greater understanding of His will.

Conclusion

Prayer is a vital aspect of the Christian faith, serving as a means of communication with God. It involves adoration, confession, thanksgiving, and supplication, aligning believers with God's will, providing peace, and fostering spiritual growth. Through prayer, believers experience communion with God, acknowledge their dependence on Him, and intercede for others. As a new believer, embracing prayer as a regular practice will deepen your relationship with God and enhance your spiritual journey.

Chapter 13: The Union with Christ

Union with Christ is a foundational concept in Christian theology that describes the profound relationship between believers and Jesus Christ. This union encompasses various dimensions, including mystical, spiritual, and legal aspects. It signifies that through faith, believers are intimately joined to Christ, sharing in His life, death, resurrection, and future glory. Here's an in-depth look at what this union means and its implications.

Union in Salvation

The New Testament frequently uses phrases like "in Christ," "with Christ," and "through Christ" to describe believers' relationship with Jesus. This union is central to salvation and Christian living.

> *"Abide in me, and I in you. As the branch cannot bear fruit by itself, unless it abides in the vine, neither can you, unless you abide in me. I am the vine; you are the branches. Whoever abides in me and I in him, he it is that bears much fruit, for apart from me you can do nothing." (John 15:4-5).*

> *"I have been crucified with Christ. It is no longer I who live, but Christ who lives in me. And the life I now live in the flesh I live by faith in the Son of God, who loved me and gave himself for me." (Galatians 2:20).*

This union implies that believers are integrally connected to Christ, drawing life and sustenance from Him, much like branches connected to a vine.

Dimensions of Union with Christ

Mystical Union:

This aspect of union with Christ emphasises the profound, spiritual connection that transcends human understanding. It reflects the mysterious and intimate relationship believers have with Jesus.

> *"This mystery is profound, and I am saying that it refers to Christ and the church." (Ephesians 5:32).*

Mystical union highlights the deep, ineffable bond that exists between Christ and His followers, a connection that goes beyond the physical realm.

Spiritual Union:

Through the Holy Spirit, believers are united with Christ in a spiritual relationship that brings new life, transformation, and sanctification.

> *"But he who is joined to the Lord becomes one spirit with him." (1 Corinthians 6:17).*

> *"You, however, are not in the flesh but in the Spirit, if in fact the Spirit of God dwells in you. Anyone who does not have the Spirit of Christ does not belong to him. But if Christ is in you,*

although the body is dead because of sin, the Spirit is life because of righteousness." (Romans 8:9-10).

Spiritual union signifies that believers are indwelt by the Holy Spirit, leading to a life that reflects Christ's righteousness and character.

Legal Union:

This dimension refers to the believer's justification through Christ. By faith, believers are legally united with Christ in His righteousness, meaning His righteous life and sacrificial death are credited to them.

"For our sake he made him to be sin who knew no sin, so that in him we might become the righteousness of God." (2 Corinthians 5:21).

"And are justified by his grace as a gift, through the redemption that is in Christ Jesus, whom God put forward as a propitiation by his blood, to be received by faith." (Romans 3:24-25).

Legal union assures believers that their sins are forgiven and that they are declared righteous before God because of Christ's atoning work.

Implications of Union with Christ

New Identity:

Believers receive a new identity in Christ. They are no longer defined by their past sins but by their new life in Him.

> *"Therefore, if anyone is in Christ, he is a new creation. The old has passed away; behold, the new has come." (2 Corinthians 5:17).*

This new identity transforms how believers view themselves and their purpose in life, rooted in their relationship with Christ.

Sanctification:

Union with Christ means ongoing transformation. Believers grow in holiness and become more like Christ through the work of the Holy Spirit.

> *"And I am sure of this, that he who began a good work in you will bring it to completion at the day of Jesus Christ." (Philippians 1:6).*

> *"For those whom he foreknew he also predestined to be conformed to the image of his Son, in order that he might be the firstborn among many brothers." (Romans 8:29).*

Sanctification is the process by which believers are progressively shaped into the likeness of Christ, reflecting His character in their lives.

Assurance of Salvation:

This union assures believers of their salvation, as their relationship with Christ guarantees their acceptance before God.

> *"I give them eternal life, and they will never perish, and no one will snatch them out of my hand. My Father, who has given them to me, is greater than all, and no one is able to snatch them out of the Father's hand." (John 10:28-29).*

Assurance of salvation provides believers with confidence and security in their eternal relationship with God.

Empowerment for Service:

Being united with Christ equips believers for service and ministry. They are empowered to live out their faith and serve others in the name of Christ.

> *"I can do all things through him who strengthens me." (Philippians 4:13).*

> *"For we are his workmanship, created in Christ Jesus for good works, which God prepared beforehand, that we should walk in them." (Ephesians 2:10).*

Empowerment for service means that believers are equipped and enabled by Christ to fulfil the good works God has planned for them.

Hope of Glory:

Union with Christ provides the hope of future glory. Believers are assured of their resurrection and eternal life with Christ.

> *"To them God chose to make known how great among the Gentiles are the riches of the glory of this mystery, which is Christ in you, the hope of glory." (Colossians 1:27).*

> *"For the Lord himself will descend from heaven with a cry of command, with the voice of an archangel, and with the sound of the trumpet of God. And the dead in Christ will rise first. Then we who are alive, who are left, will be caught up together with them in the clouds to meet the Lord in the air, and so we will always be with the Lord." (1 Thessalonians 4:16-17).*

The hope of glory assures believers of their ultimate destiny and eternal life with Christ.

Conclusion

Union with Christ is a multifaceted doctrine that encompasses the believer's mystical, spiritual, and legal connection to Jesus. This union results in a new identity, ongoing sanctification, assurance of salvation, empowerment for service, and the hope of eternal glory. Rooted in Scripture, this profound relationship underscores the centrality of Christ in every aspect of the believer's life. Understanding and embracing this union is crucial for growing in faith and experiencing the fullness of the Christian life.

Chapter 14: Understanding and Application for Followers of Jesus

The Great Commandment

The Great Commandment is a central teaching of Jesus that underscores the paramount importance of love in the life of a believer. Found in the Gospels of Matthew, Mark, and Luke, this teaching encapsulates the essence of the Law and the Prophets, highlighting love for God and neighbour as the core of Christian living.

"And he said to him, 'You shall love the Lord your God with all your heart and with all your soul and with all your mind. This is the great and first commandment. And a second is like it: You shall love your neighbour as yourself. On these two commandments depend all the Law and the Prophets.'" (Matthew 22:37-40).

"'And you shall love the Lord your God with all your heart and with all your soul and with all your mind and with all your strength.' The second is this: 'You shall love your neighbour as yourself.' There is no other commandment greater than these." (Mark 12:30-31).

Components of the Great Commandment

Love God

Believers are called to love God with their entire being—heart, soul, mind, and strength. This complete devotion involves a holistic commitment to God, encompassing emotional, spiritual, intellectual, and physical dedication.

> *"You shall love the Lord your God with all your heart and with all your soul and with all your might." (Deuteronomy 6:5).*

This commandment requires believers to prioritise their relationship with God above all else, seeking to know Him deeply, worship Him sincerely, and obey His commands fully. It is a call to an intimate and personal relationship with the Creator, marked by reverence, adoration, and submission.

Love Your Neighbour

Loving one's neighbour as oneself means demonstrating genuine care, empathy, and kindness towards others. It involves treating others with the same respect and consideration that one would wish for oneself.

> *"You shall not take vengeance or bear a grudge against the sons of your own people, but you*

shall love your neighbour as yourself: I am the Lord." (Leviticus 19:18).

This command extends beyond mere tolerance or passive benevolence; it calls for active engagement in acts of mercy, justice, and compassion. It challenges believers to look beyond their own needs and interests, reaching out to others in love, even when it is inconvenient or costly.

Application for Followers of Jesus

Personal Devotion

Believers are encouraged to prioritise their personal relationship with God through regular prayer, study of Scripture, and worship. These practices nurture a deeper love for God and align the believer's heart with His will.

Obedience

Living according to God's commandments and teachings is an expression of love for Him. Obedience to God's Word reflects a commitment to His authority and a desire to honour Him in all aspects of life.

Service to Others

Engaging in acts of kindness, justice, and mercy is a tangible expression of love for one's neighbour. Believers are called to serve others selflessly, treating them with dignity and respect, and advocating for their well-being.

Community Involvement

Participation in the life of the church and local community provides opportunities to demonstrate God's love collectively. By serving within the church and engaging in community outreach, believers can embody the love of Christ and foster a sense of unity and support.

The Great Commission

The Great Commission is Jesus' mandate to His disciples to spread the gospel and make disciples of all nations. This command underscores the global and missional aspect of the Christian faith, calling believers to be proactive in evangelism and discipleship.

> *"And Jesus came and said to them, 'All authority in heaven and on earth has been given to me. Go therefore and make disciples of all nations, baptising them in the name of the Father and of the Son and of the Holy Spirit, teaching them to observe all that I have commanded you. And behold, I am with you always, to the end of the age.'" (Matthew 28:18-20).*

Components of the Great Commission

Go

Jesus commands His followers to go into the world, signifying intentionality and a willingness to step out of one's comfort zone. This involves crossing cultural, geographical, and social boundaries to share the gospel.

> *"But you will receive power when the Holy Spirit has come upon you, and you will be my witnesses in Jerusalem and in all Judea and Samaria, and to the end of the earth." (Acts 1:8).*

This command challenges believers to be active and engaged in their mission, seeking out opportunities to witness to others about the love and salvation found in Jesus Christ.

Make Disciples

The heart of the Great Commission is the making of disciples, which involves more than just evangelism. It requires teaching, discipling, and nurturing new believers to grow in their faith and obedience to Christ.

> *"And what you have heard from me in the presence of many witnesses entrust to faithful men who will be able to teach others also." (2 Timothy 2:2).*

Discipleship is an ongoing process that involves helping others to understand and apply biblical truths, fostering spiritual maturity, and encouraging a deep and abiding relationship with Jesus.

Baptising

Baptism is a significant and public declaration of faith, symbolising the believer's identification with Christ's death, burial, and resurrection. It represents a new life in Christ and entry into the Christian community.

> *"Do you not know that all of us who have been baptised into Christ Jesus were baptised into his death? We were buried therefore with him by baptism into death, in order that, just as Christ was raised from the dead by the glory of the Father, we too might walk in newness of life."* (Romans 6:3-4).

Teaching

Teaching new believers to observe Christ's commandments is essential for their spiritual growth and maturity. This involves imparting biblical knowledge, wisdom, and practical application of Scripture.

> *"Him we proclaim, warning everyone and teaching everyone with all wisdom, that we may present everyone mature in Christ." (Colossians 1:28).*

Application for Followers of Jesus

Evangelism

Believers are called to share the gospel with others, both locally and globally. This can involve personal conversations, supporting missionary efforts, and using various media to spread the message. Effective evangelism requires sensitivity, respect, and a genuine love for those who are being reached.

Discipleship

Investing in the spiritual growth of others is a critical aspect of the Great Commission. This includes discipling new believers, leading Bible studies, and providing ongoing support and guidance. Discipleship fosters a community of believers who are equipped to grow in their faith and disciple others in turn.

Baptism

Encouraging and participating in the baptism of new believers is a public testament to their faith. Baptism services provide an opportunity for the church community to celebrate and support new members as they take this significant step in their spiritual journey.

Teaching

Continual learning and teaching of God's Word are vital for the health and growth of the Christian community. Believers should engage in lifelong learning, study Scripture diligently, and help others to understand and apply biblical teachings.

Conclusion

The Great Commandment and the Great Commission are foundational to the Christian faith and practice. The Great Commandment calls believers to love God wholly and to love others selflessly, forming the basis of Christian ethics and relationships. The Great Commission charges believers with the responsibility to spread the gospel, make disciples, and teach obedience to Christ's commands. Together, these mandates shape the mission and purpose of the Christian life, guiding believers in their personal devotion, community involvement, and global outreach. Following Jesus means embracing these commands and actively participating in God's redemptive work in the world. Through loving God and others, and by making disciples of all nations, believers fulfil their divine calling and contribute to the advancement of God's Kingdom.

Chapter 15: Understanding Sin and Falling Away in the Christian Faith

What Happens If You Sin?

Even as Christians, sinning remains an unfortunate reality due to the ongoing struggle with the sinful nature. However, the Bible offers assurance and guidance for dealing with sin.

Confession and Forgiveness

When believers sin, they are called to confess their sins to God, who is faithful to forgive and cleanse them from all unrighteousness.

> *"If we confess our sins, he is faithful and just to forgive us our sins and to cleanse us from all unrighteousness." (1 John 1:9).*

> *"Whoever conceals his transgressions will not prosper, but he who confesses and forsakes them will obtain mercy." (Proverbs 28:13).*

Repentance

True repentance involves a heartfelt change and a turning away from sin, seeking to live a life that pleases God.

"Repent therefore, and turn back, that your sins may be blotted out, that times of refreshing may come from the presence of the Lord." (Acts 3:19).

"For godly grief produces a repentance that leads to salvation without regret, whereas worldly grief produces death." (2 Corinthians 7:10).

Assurance of Forgiveness

Believers can be confident in God's promise of forgiveness through Jesus Christ.

"There is therefore now no condemnation for those who are in Christ Jesus." (Romans 8:1).

"As far as the east is from the west, so far does he remove our transgressions from us." (Psalm 103:12).

What Happens If You Fall Away?

The concept of falling away, or apostasy, raises significant concerns about salvation and perseverance in the Christian faith. Here are key points to consider:

Perseverance of the Saints

Scripture holds that true believers will persevere in their faith until the end. This doctrine is known as the perseverance of the saints.

"I give them eternal life, and they will never perish, and no one will snatch them out of my hand. My Father, who has given them to me, is greater than all, and no one is able to snatch them out of the Father's hand." (John 10:28-29).

"And I am sure of this, that he who began a good work in you will bring it to completion at the day of Jesus Christ." (Philippians 1:6).

Evidence of Genuine Faith

A true believer's life will exhibit evidence of genuine faith through ongoing repentance, growth in holiness, and the fruit of the Spirit.

"Thus you will recognise them by their fruits." (Matthew 7:20).

"But the fruit of the Spirit is love, joy, peace, patience, kindness, goodness, faithfulness, gentleness, self-control; against such things there is no law." (Galatians 5:22-23).

Warnings Against Falling Away

The Bible contains warnings against falling away to encourage believers to remain faithful and vigilant in their walk with Christ.

"For it is impossible, in the case of those who have once been enlightened, who have tasted the heavenly gift, and have shared in the Holy Spirit, and have tasted the goodness of the word of God and the powers of the age to come, and

then have fallen away, to restore them again to repentance, since they are crucifying once again the Son of God to their own harm and holding him up to contempt." (Hebrews 6:4-6).

"Therefore let anyone who thinks that he stands take heed lest he fall." (1 Corinthians 10:12).

Restoration

If a believer stumbles or backslides, restoration is possible through repentance and seeking God's grace.

"My brothers, if anyone among you wanders from the truth and someone brings him back, let him know that whoever brings back a sinner from his wandering will save his soul from death and will cover a multitude of sins." (James 5:19-20).

"Brothers, if anyone is caught in any transgression, you who are spiritual should restore him in a spirit of gentleness. Keep watch on yourself, lest you too be tempted." (Galatians 6:1).

Assurance and Encouragement

For those concerned about their spiritual state, it is essential to hold on to God's promises and seek reassurance through Scripture and prayer.

God's Faithfulness

God is faithful to His promises and will not abandon His children.

> *"If we are faithless, he remains faithful—for he cannot deny himself." (2 Timothy 2:13).*

Seeking God

Continuously seek God through prayer, Scripture, and fellowship with other believers to strengthen your faith and commitment.

> *"You will seek me and find me, when you seek me with all your heart." (Jeremiah 29:13).*

> *"Not neglecting to meet together, as is the habit of some, but encouraging one another, and all the more as you see the Day drawing near." (Hebrews 10:25).*

Conclusion

Sin and falling away are serious concerns, but the Bible provides a path to restoration through confession, repentance, and faith in Jesus Christ. Genuine believers are assured of God's faithfulness and their perseverance in faith. Continual growth, vigilance, and reliance on God's grace are vital in maintaining a strong and enduring relationship with Him. If you stumble, remember that God's grace is sufficient, and restoration is always possible through repentance and seeking

His forgiveness. By holding on to His promises and remaining committed to a life of faith, believers can experience the fullness of God's love and grace.

Conclusion: Embracing the Fullness of the Christian Life

As we conclude this journey through understanding key aspects of the Christian faith, it's essential to underscore the importance of community and discipleship. Joining a church is not merely about attending services; it is about becoming part of a spiritual family where you can grow, serve, and be nurtured in your faith.

The Role of the Church

The church plays a vital role in the life of a believer. It is a place where you can receive sound teaching, participate in meaningful worship, and engage in fellowship with other believers. Hebrews 10:25 encourages us, *"Not neglecting to meet together, as is the habit of some, but encouraging one another, and all the more as you see the Day drawing near."* Being an active member of a church community helps to reinforce your faith, provides accountability, and offers opportunities for service and spiritual growth.

The Importance of Discipleship

Discipleship is a crucial element of the Christian life. It involves being discipled and discipling others, learning and teaching the truths of the faith, and growing in spiritual maturity. Jesus' Great

Commission commands us to "go and make disciples of all nations" (Matthew 28:19). This is a lifelong journey of learning, applying biblical principles, and helping others to do the same. Through discipleship, you can deepen your understanding of God's word, develop your spiritual gifts, and strengthen your walk with Christ.

Resting in the Finished Work of Christ

The Christian life is not about striving through our own efforts or being driven by fleeting emotions. Instead, it is about resting in the finished work of Christ. On the cross, Jesus declared, *"It is finished"* (John 19:30), signifying that the work of salvation was complete. Our role is to trust in this completed work and live out our faith with the assurance that our salvation is secure, not by our works, but by God's grace. Ephesians 2:8-9 reminds us, *"For by grace you have been saved through faith. And this is not your own doing; it is the gift of God, not a result of works, so that no one may boast."*

Being Led and Empowered by the Holy Spirit

The Holy Spirit is our helper, guide, and source of strength. As believers, we are called to live lives led and empowered by the Holy Spirit. Galatians 5:16 encourages us to *"walk by the Spirit, and you will not gratify the desires of the flesh."* The Spirit helps us to understand God's word, convicts us of sin, and empowers us to live righteously. By relying on the Holy Spirit, we can experience the fullness of the Christian life, marked by love, joy, peace, and all the fruits of the Spirit (Galatians 5:22-23).

A Call to Action

In light of these truths, I encourage you to take the next step in your spiritual journey. If you are not already part of a church, seek out a local congregation where you can belong and grow. Engage in discipleship, both receiving and giving guidance, to foster spiritual maturity. Remember, your faith is not about feelings or works; it is about resting in the finished work of Christ and being led by the Holy Spirit.

Embrace this journey with confidence, knowing that God's grace is sufficient, and His Spirit is with you every step of the way. As you integrate into the life of the church and commit to discipleship, you will discover the richness and depth of a life lived for God's glory. Trust in His promises, rely on His strength, and walk in the fullness of His love and grace.

Join Theology School

Dear friend,

Thank you for your interest in participating in a Bible study! We're excited to meet you and explore God's Word with you. Please take a moment to provide us with some information, and we will contact you shortly to discuss further details.

Name:

_____

Email:

_____

Phone Number:

_____

Preferred Method(s) of Communication:
(Select all that apply)

☐ Email　　　☐ Phone　　　☐ WhatsApp

☐ Other (Please specify)

_____

Availability: (Specify days and times that work best for you)

_____

_____

_____

Briefly share your background and any specific areas of interest or questions you have regarding the Bible:

_____

_____

_____

We are excited to meet you and begin this journey of studying God's Word with you. Our goal is to create a welcoming and supportive environment where we can deepen our faith and grow in our understanding of Scripture.

If you have any immediate questions or concerns, please feel free to reach out to us at info@theologyschool.org. We'll do our best to assist you promptly.

Thank you once again for your interest, and we can't wait to begin this Bible study journey together!

Blessings,

Theology School International
www.theologyschool.org

Printed in Great Britain
by Amazon

44184110R00057